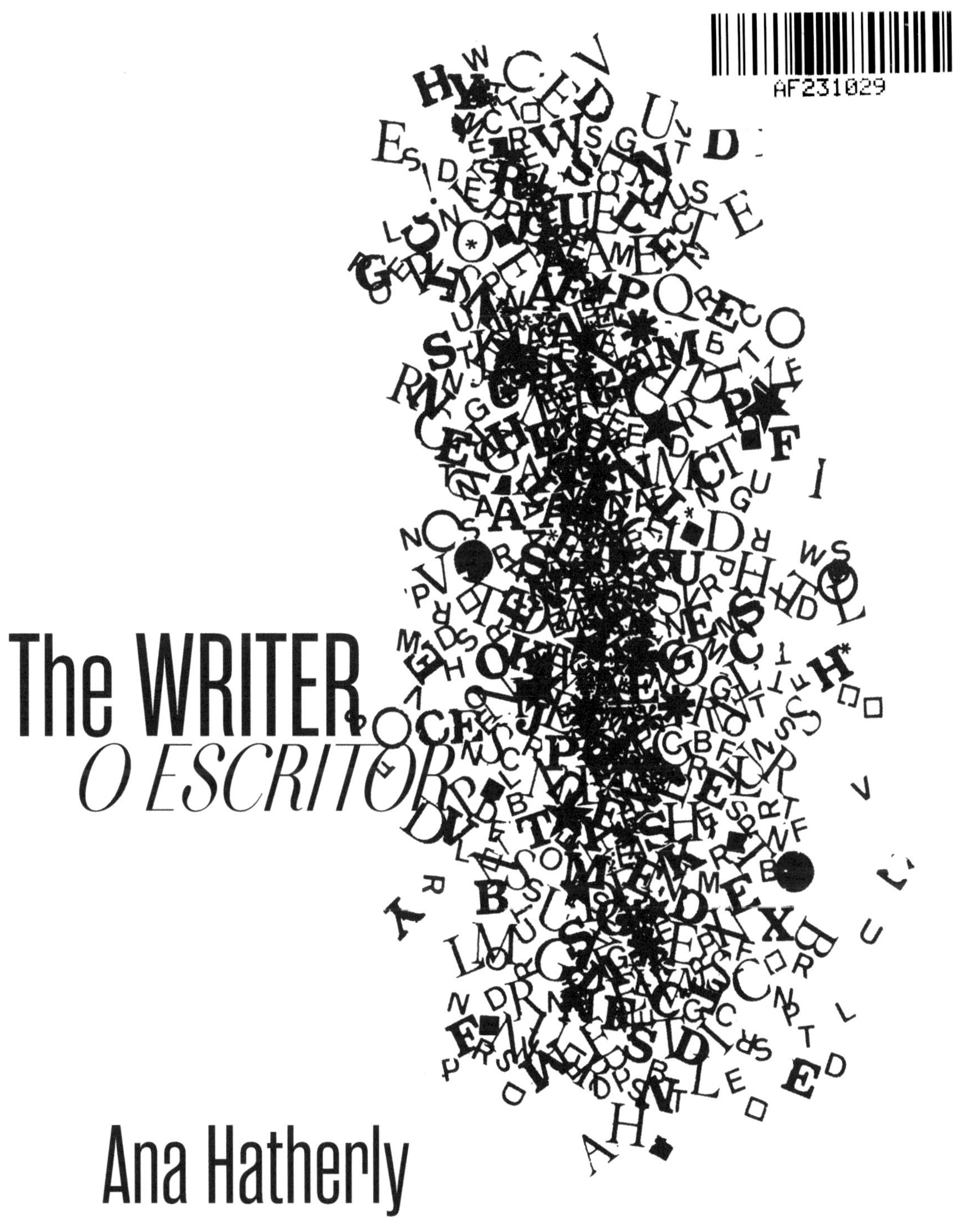

The WRITER
O ESCRITOR

Ana Hatherly

Introduction **Tim Gaze**

Translation Dr Maria Luísa Coelho

Hysterical Books
Asemia Editions

Introduction
Tim Gaze

Author's Introduction
translated from the Portuguese
Dr Maria Luísa Coelho
Camões Portuguese Lecturer
Faculty of Medieval and Modern Languages
University of Oxford

The images for this book were scanned from the original print edition *O Escritor* by Ana Hatherly, copyright ©1975, as part of the Círculo de poesia series produced by Moraes Editores, Lisbon.

Grateful Acknowledgement is made to Moraes Editores. Special Thanks to Sociedade Portuguesa de Autores for helping us gain permission.

Permission to publish granted by Dra. Teresa Pestana, legal representative for the estate of Ana Hatherly.

The Writer, by Ana Hatherly
Hysterical Books © 2025

ISBN 978-0-940821-34-7
Library of Congress Control Number: 2025942946

Tim Gaze, Editor
Translation by Dr Maria Luísa Coelho
Kristine Snodgrass, Curator
Design by Jay Snodgrass

Hysterical Books
hystericalbooks.com
1506 Wekewa Nene
Tallahassee, Florida 32301

Hysterical Books
Asemia Editions

THE WRITER
O Escritor

1967-2025

ANA HATHERLY

O Escritor ("The Writer") by Ana Hatherly (1929–2015) was originally published by Moraes Editores of Lisbon, as part of their Círculo de Poesia series, in 1975. My vision was to manifest a new edition of this work, by an author and poet renowned in Lusophone culture, but little-known in the English-speaking world. I first learned of O Escritor at the blog The Crib Sheet, by comics scholar Domingos Isabelinho. As an enthusiast for asemic writing (that is, material that resembles writing, but which can't be conventionally read), I consider Hatherly to be an important part of its history, deserving equal billing with the likes of Mirtha Dermisache and Henri Michaux.

For the Hysterical Books edition, we translated the title as The Writer and offer a new translation of the author's introduction, for easier access to English language readers. The book, while appearing to be simple, seems to be about the difficulties the writer faces in communicating clear meaning in speech and written language.

In addition to her output in the literary arts, Ana was a painter and film-maker. There is an obvious synergy between her writing and her visual creativity. Many of her works can be freely seen at the Portuguese experimental poetry site PO-EX (https://po-ex.net/). For an excellent overview of her career, see Natalie Ferris's 'The Intelligent Hand: Ana Hatherly / Asemic Writing / Visualizing the Creative Act' (https://modernismmodernity.org/forums/posts/ferris-intelligent-hand-ana-hatherly). Much of her radical creativity occurred during the regime of the dictator Salazar, which ended in 1974.

Ana's English surname Hatherly deserves explaining. Her surname at birth was Alves (full name Ana Maria de Lourdes Rocha Alves). In 1952, she married an English businessman named Henry Hatherly, adopting his surname.

50 years since the original publication, in 2025, is an appropriate time for this new edition to appear. May it find appreciative new readers!

I wish to thank Drª Teresa Pestana, Dr Maria Luísa Coelho, Domingos Isabelinho, Fernando Aguiar and Kristine & Jay Snodgrass.

Tim Gaze
June 2025

«O Escritor» é um narrativa em 27 fases. Cada imagem é um pictograma, um fotograma congelado na página, cujo significado é posto em movimento pela leitura. A leitura será sempre múltipla porque à ilusão de ver se acrescenta a ilusão de ler. Todo o pictograma é criptograma.

A história da imaginação é também a história do seu vocabulário e este implica aquilo a que Coleridge chamou «a voluntária suspensão da descrença».

Entre o autor e o leitor cria-se uma relação de cumplicidade: possuídos dum código comum decifram-se mutuamente.

É assim que se instituem.

O autor e o leitor são exploradores sistemáticos—o autor fornece o mapa dos itinerários e o leitor percorre-os, mas os percursos são livremente condicionados.

O autor concebe o percurso da experiência e realiza-o primeiro mas ao publicá-lo deturpa-o, isto é, transfigura-o, e desse modo a sua experiência o ultrapassa.

É nesse instante que ele adquire o valor de documento pois que referindo-se a ele refere-se a ela: a publicação resume uma série de actos, os quais, por si, referem uma multidão de coexistências. Se para o autor a publicação é a última fase do processo, para a obra ela é a primeira, e assim tão documental é a publicação da sua experiência como a interpretação que dela hão-de fazer os leitores.

Translated By Dr Maria Luísa Coelho

"The Writer" is a narrative in 27 phases. Each image is a pictogram, a frozen photogram on the page, whose meaning is set in motion by reading. Reading will always be multiple because the illusion of seeing is compounded by the illusion of reading. Every pictogram is a cryptogram.

The history of the imagination is also the history of its vocabulary, which implies what Coleridge called "the willing suspension of disbelief."

A relationship of complicity is created between the author and the reader: possessed of a common code, they decipher each other.

That is how they establish themselves.

The author and the reader are systematic explorers—the author provides the map of itineraries and the reader traverses them, but the journeys are freely conditioned.

The author conceives the journey of the experience and first carries it out, but upon publishing it, she distorts it, that is, she transfigures it, and in this way, her experience surpasses it.

It's in that moment that the journey acquires the value of a document because, in referring to her, it refers to the experience: the publication sums up a series of acts, which, in themselves, reference a multitude of coexistences. If for the author, publication is the last phase of the process, for the work, it is the first, and in this way, both the publication of her experience and the interpretation that readers will make of it are equally documentary.

«O Escritor» documenta, simultaneamente, um percurso e a sua petrificação no texto, o modo como este se autonomiza, o modo como aquele nele desaparece: o modo como o escritor substitui a fala pela escrita, que é a sua voz mais alta, mais ambígua.

É assim que os diferentes graus de legibilidade do texto se tornam um desafio à construção de significados.

O leitor torna-se uma testemunha que depõe, agindo, nesse processo histórico.

«O Escritor», elaborado entre 1967 e 1972, pode dizer-se particularmente característico da fase difícil que atravessaram alguns escritores portugueses da geração da autora em que o desânimo e a descrença e, por outro lado, a revolta e a repulsa, ao mesmo tempo que os impeliam a prosseguir minavam o seu trabalho. Nesse aspecto é também uma representação necessária dum estado de repressão prolongada.

A.H.

Janeiro de 1975.

"The Writer" simultaneously documents a journey and its petrification in the text, the way the text becomes autonomous, the way the journey disappears within it: the way the writer replaces speech with writing, which is her loudest, most ambiguous voice.

That is how the different degrees of legibility of the text become a challenge in the construction of meanings.

The reader becomes a witness who testifies, by acting, in that historical process.

"The Writer", developed between 1967 and 1972, can be said to be particularly characteristic of the difficult phase experienced by some Portuguese writers of the author's generation, in which dejection and disbelief, on the one hand, and revolt and revulsion, on the other, both drove them forward and undermined their work. In that sense, it is also a necessary representation of a state of prolonged repression.

A.H.

January 1975.

ANA HATHERLY

THE WRITER

(1967–2025)

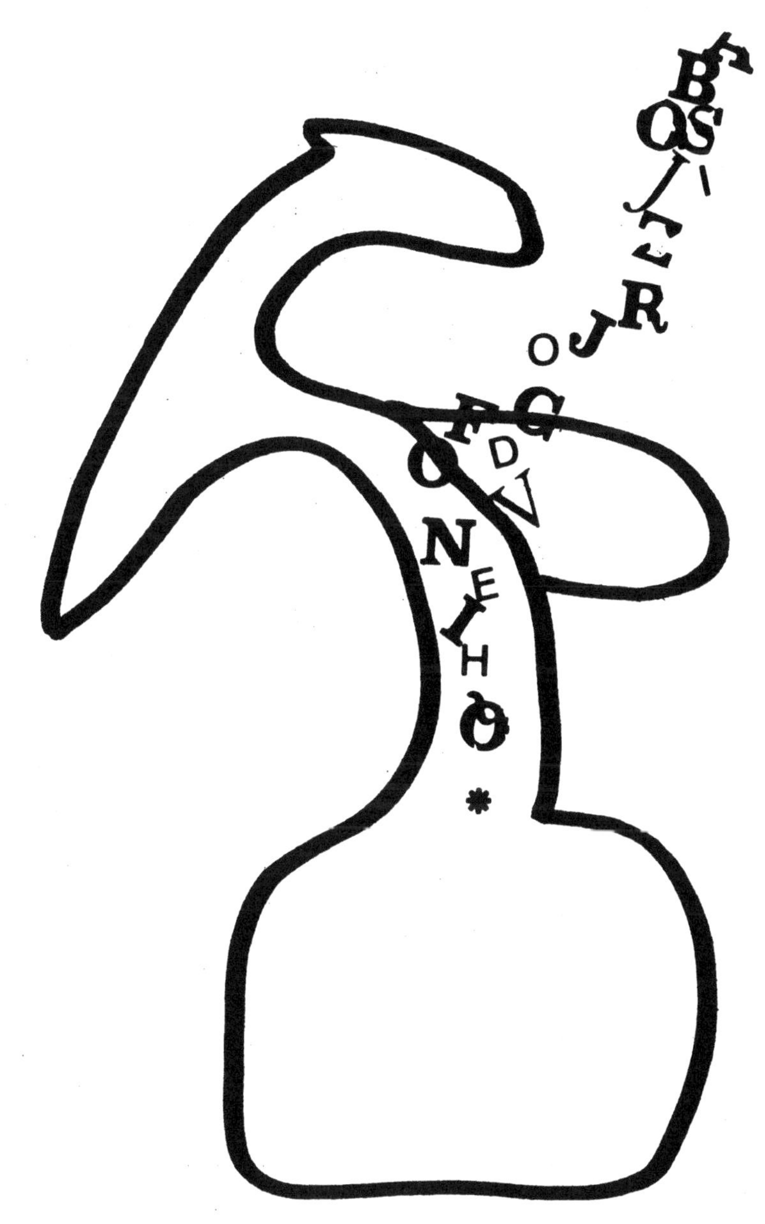

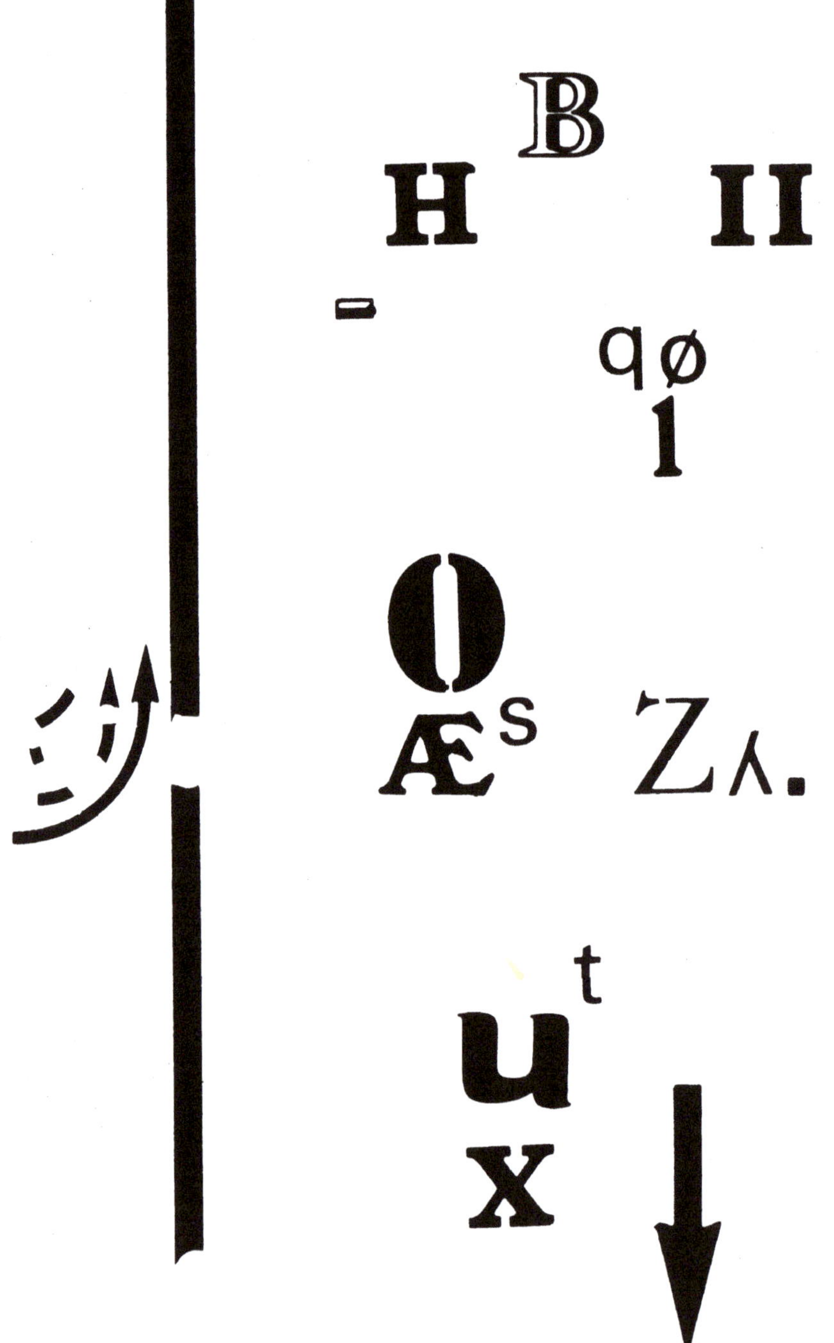

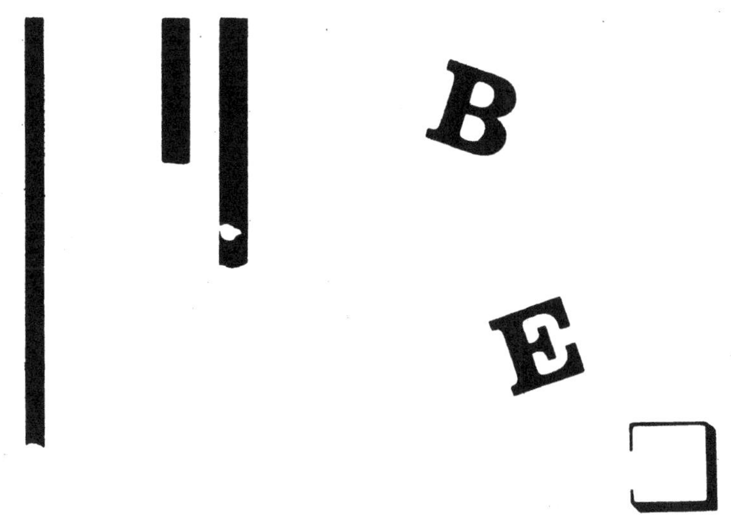

B
E
O!
II
KPYOTL

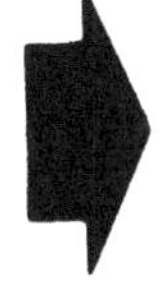

RU?

mNåå

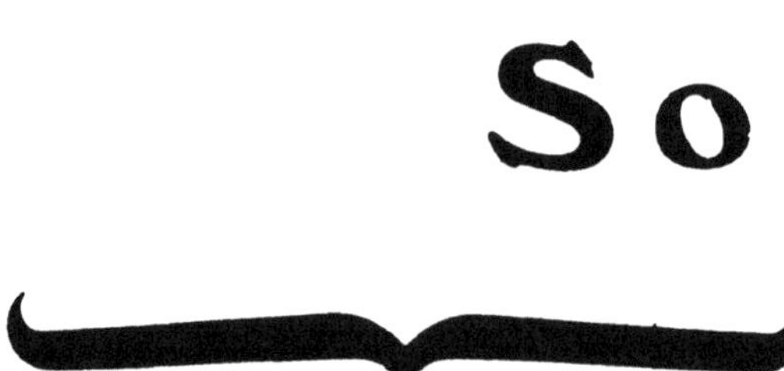

So

LUPQ

moRLU?

7

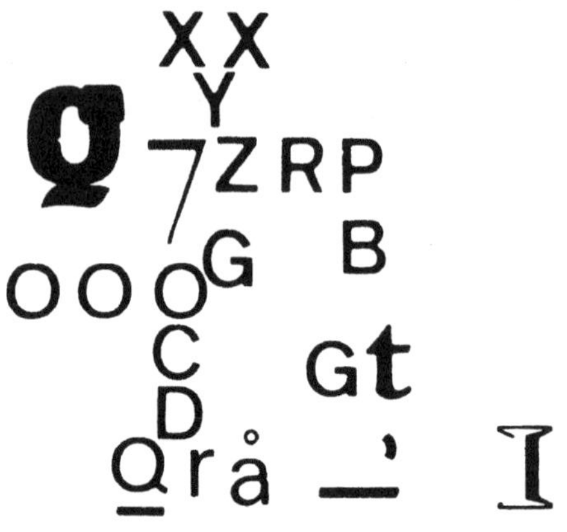

T
H
R R E E E E H J H H
E F
H L
|
|
g.

N O ?

C W Z
M
O
6 un ß
_ J.

tf°   9σ

ø g h

(IrQ)

ZØ_T

ä à?

I

ü1 →

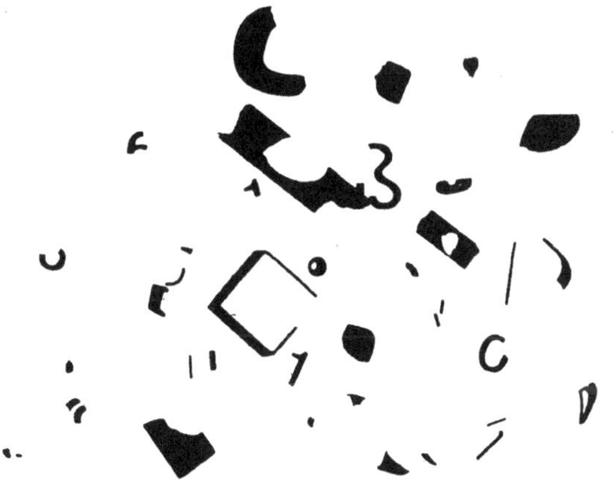

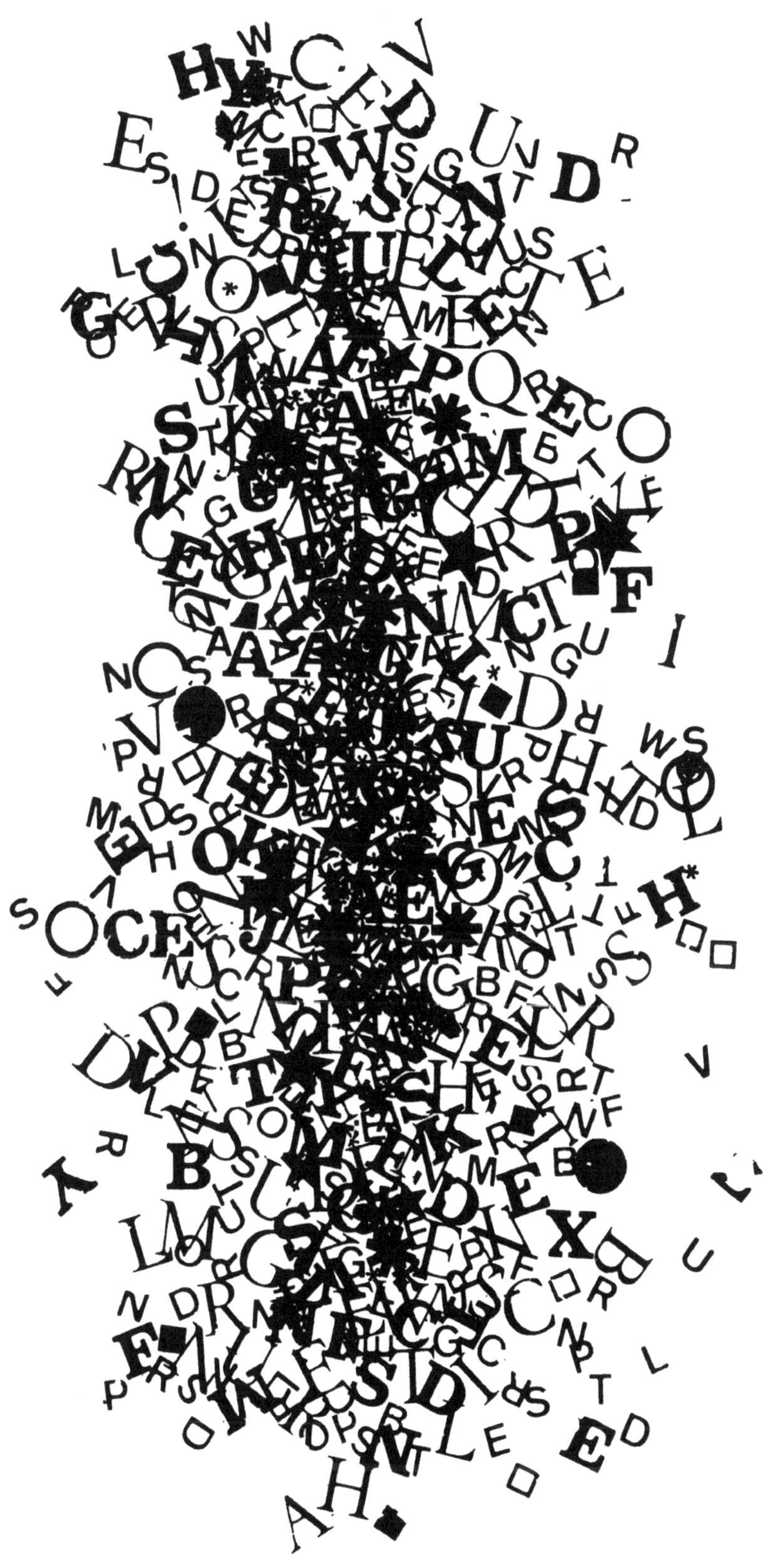

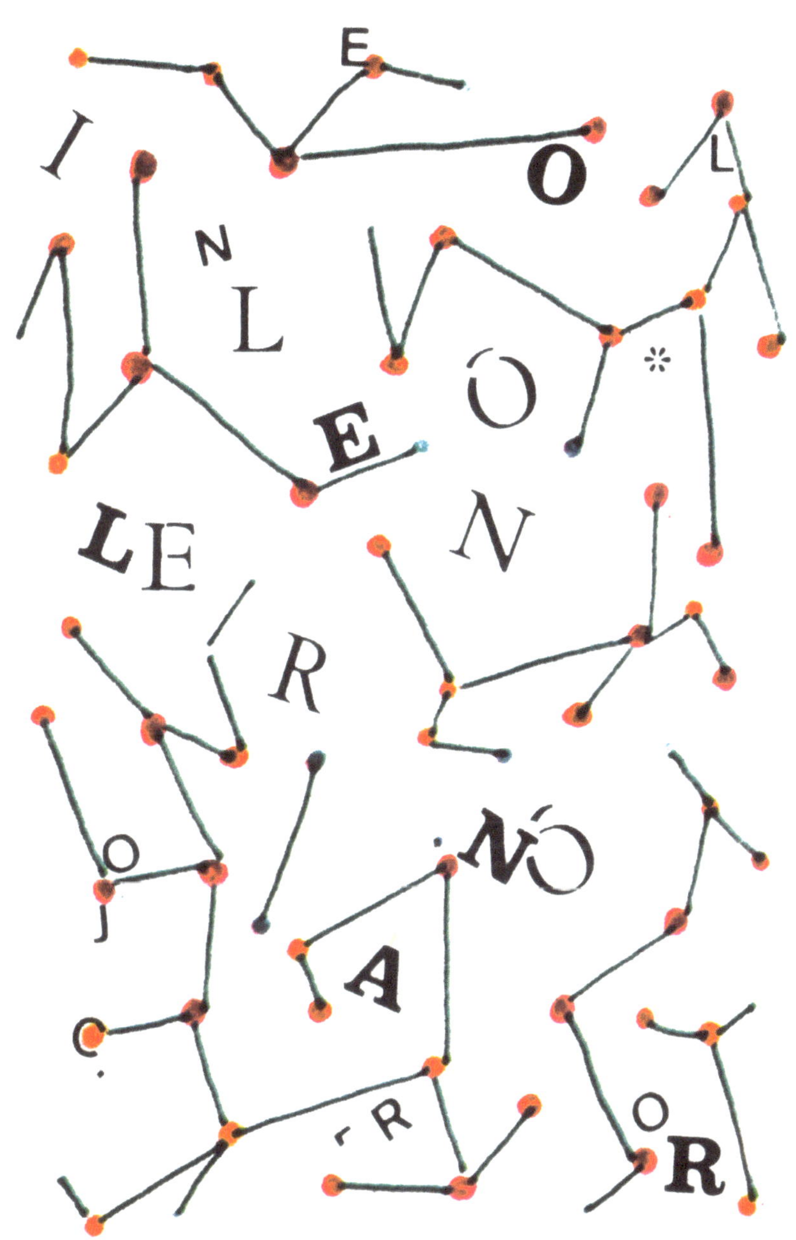

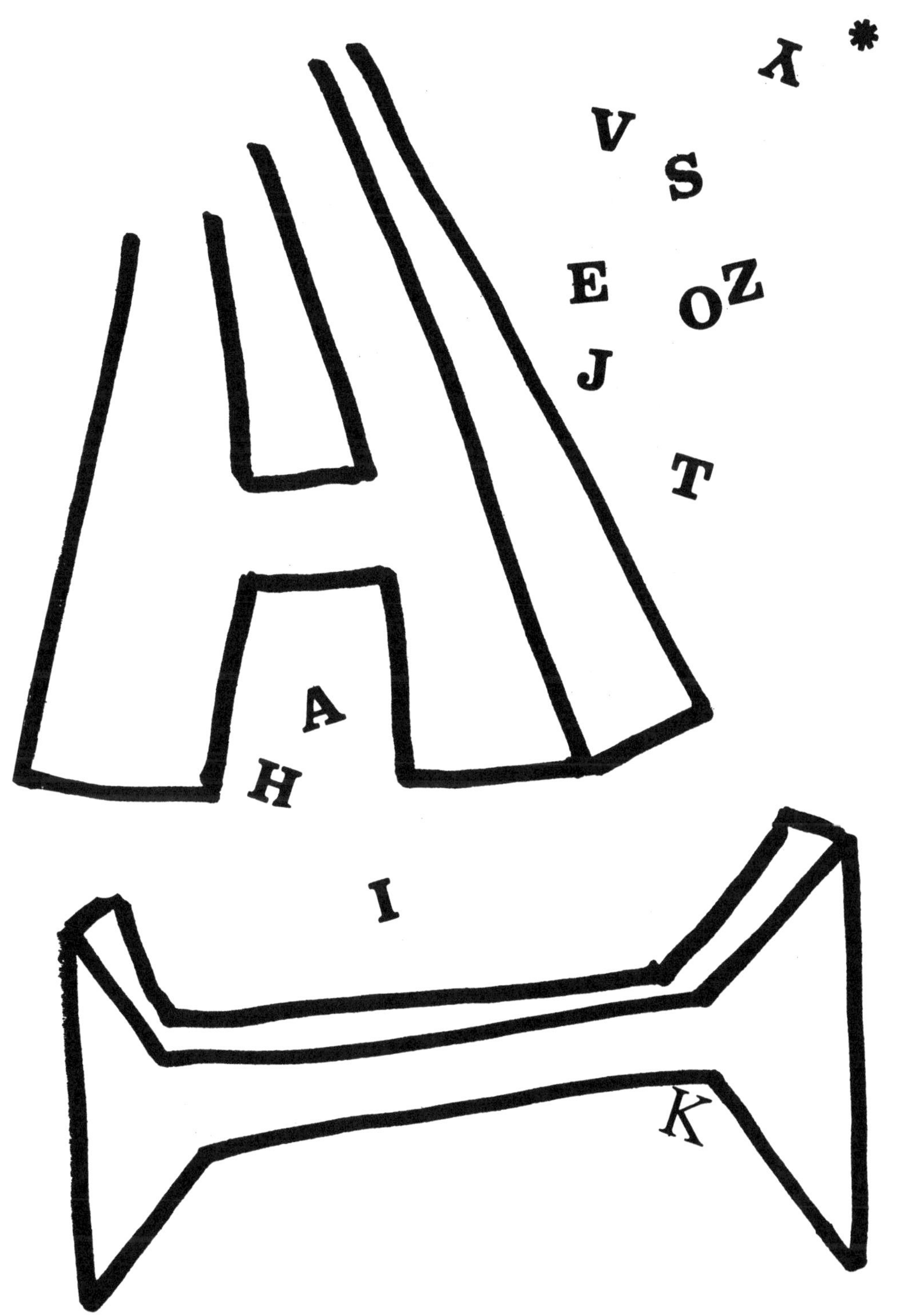

Y
*
V
S
E
O
Z
J
T
A
H
I
K

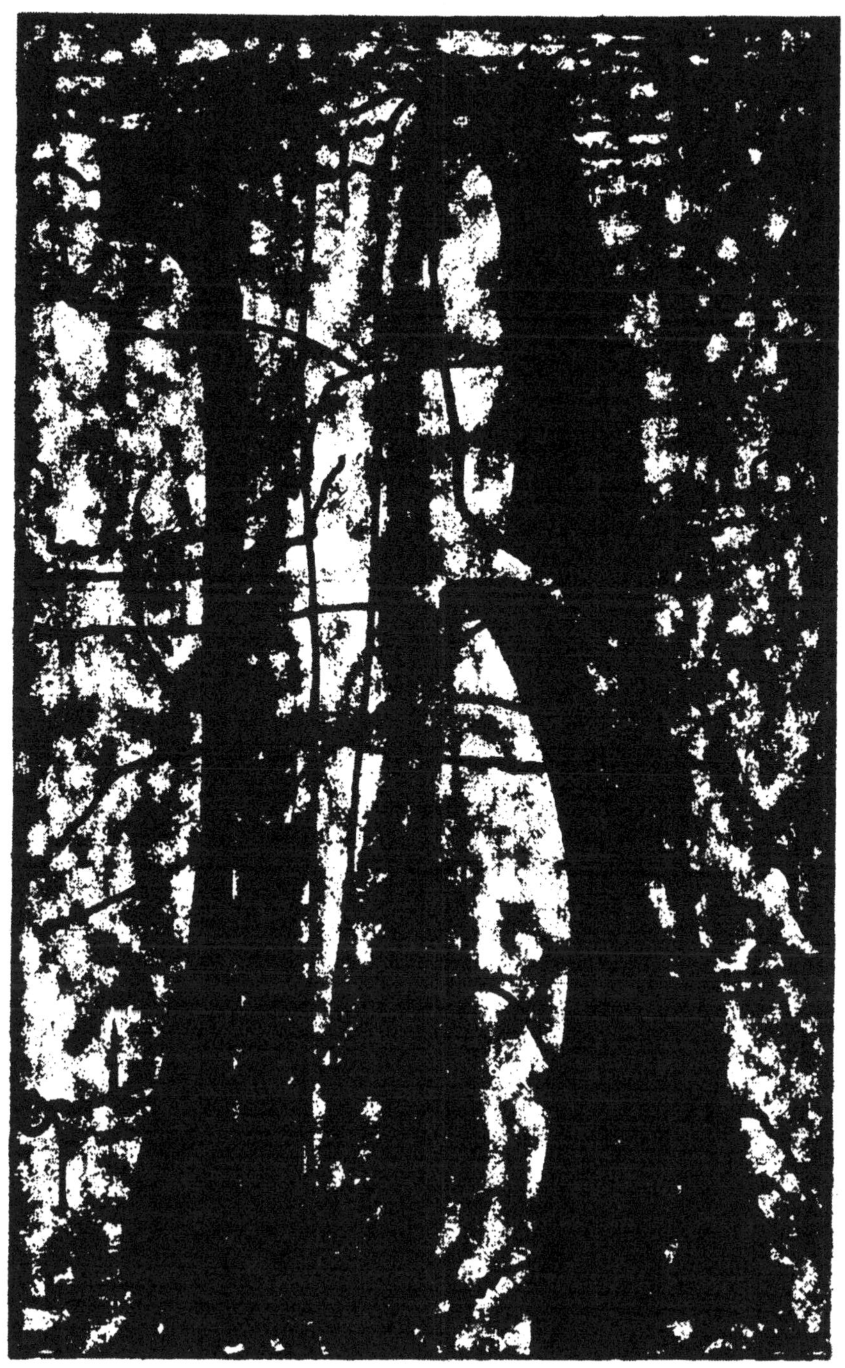

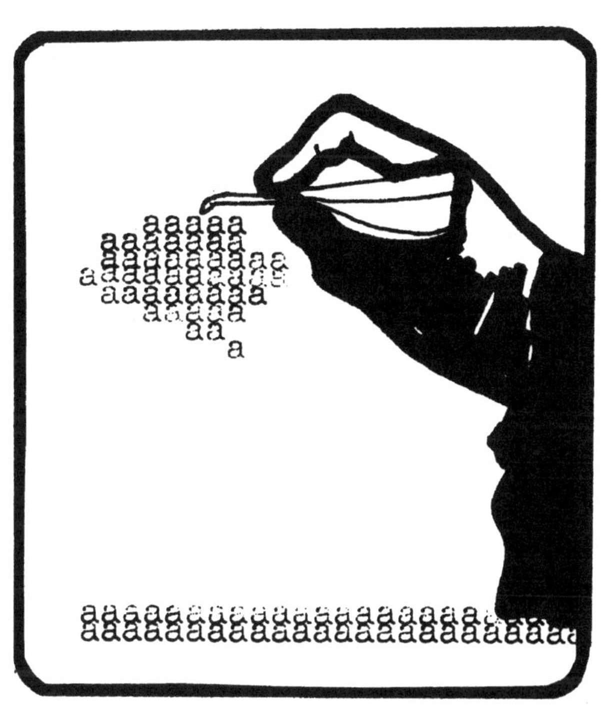

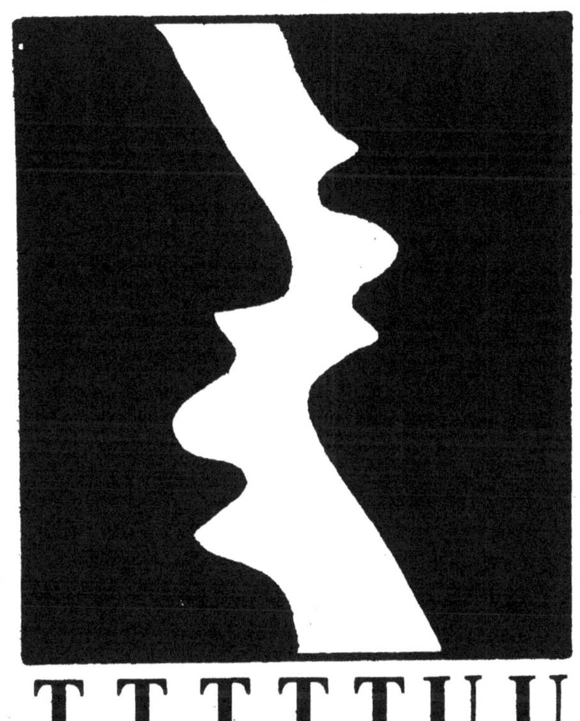

TTTTTUU

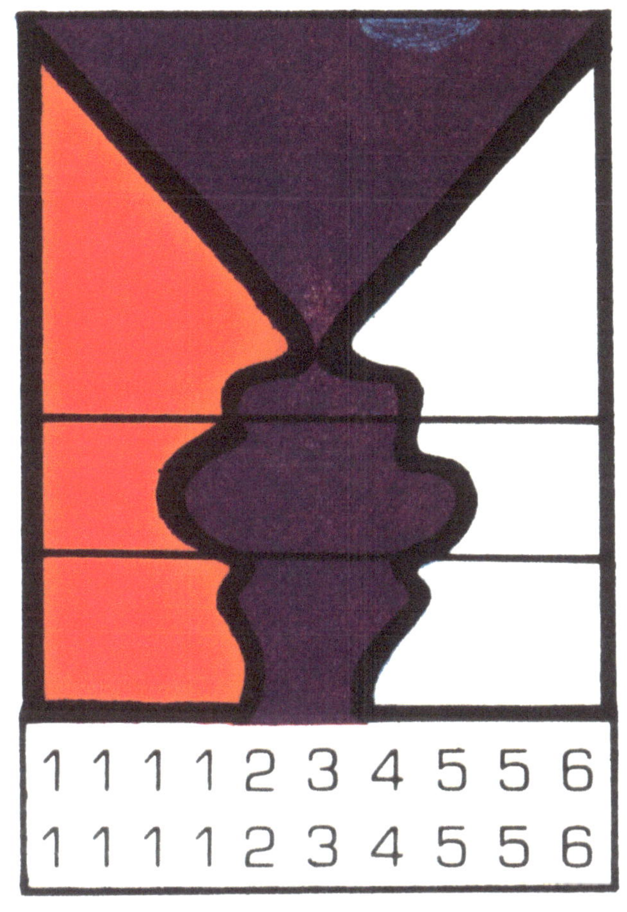

1 1 1 1 2 3 4 5 5 6
1 1 1 1 2 3 4 5 5 6

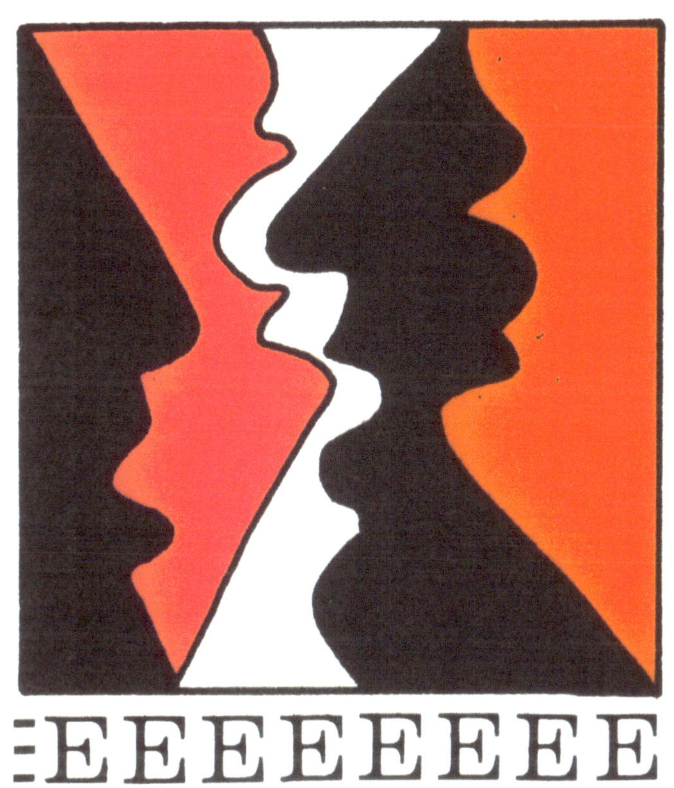

EEEEEEEEEE

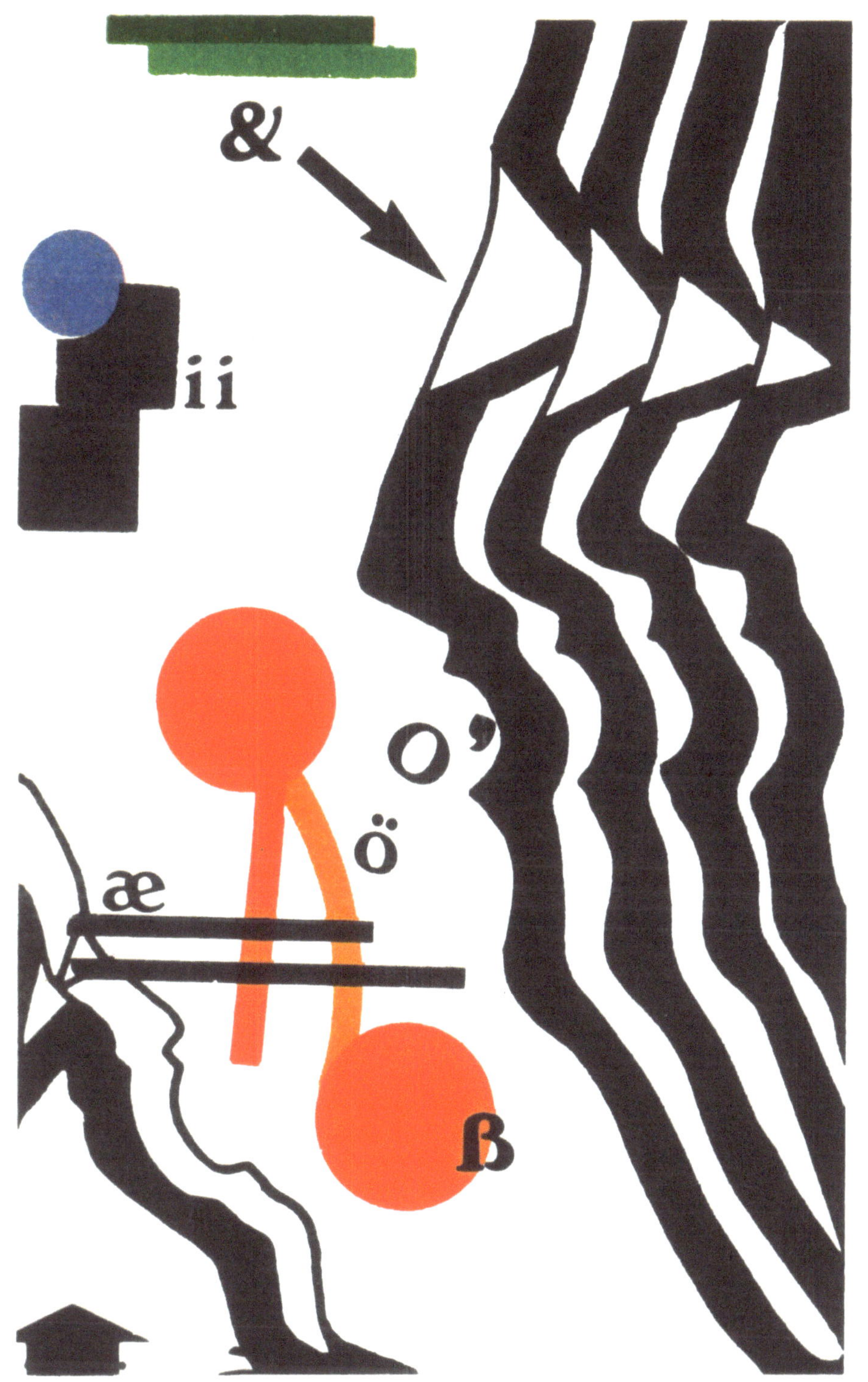

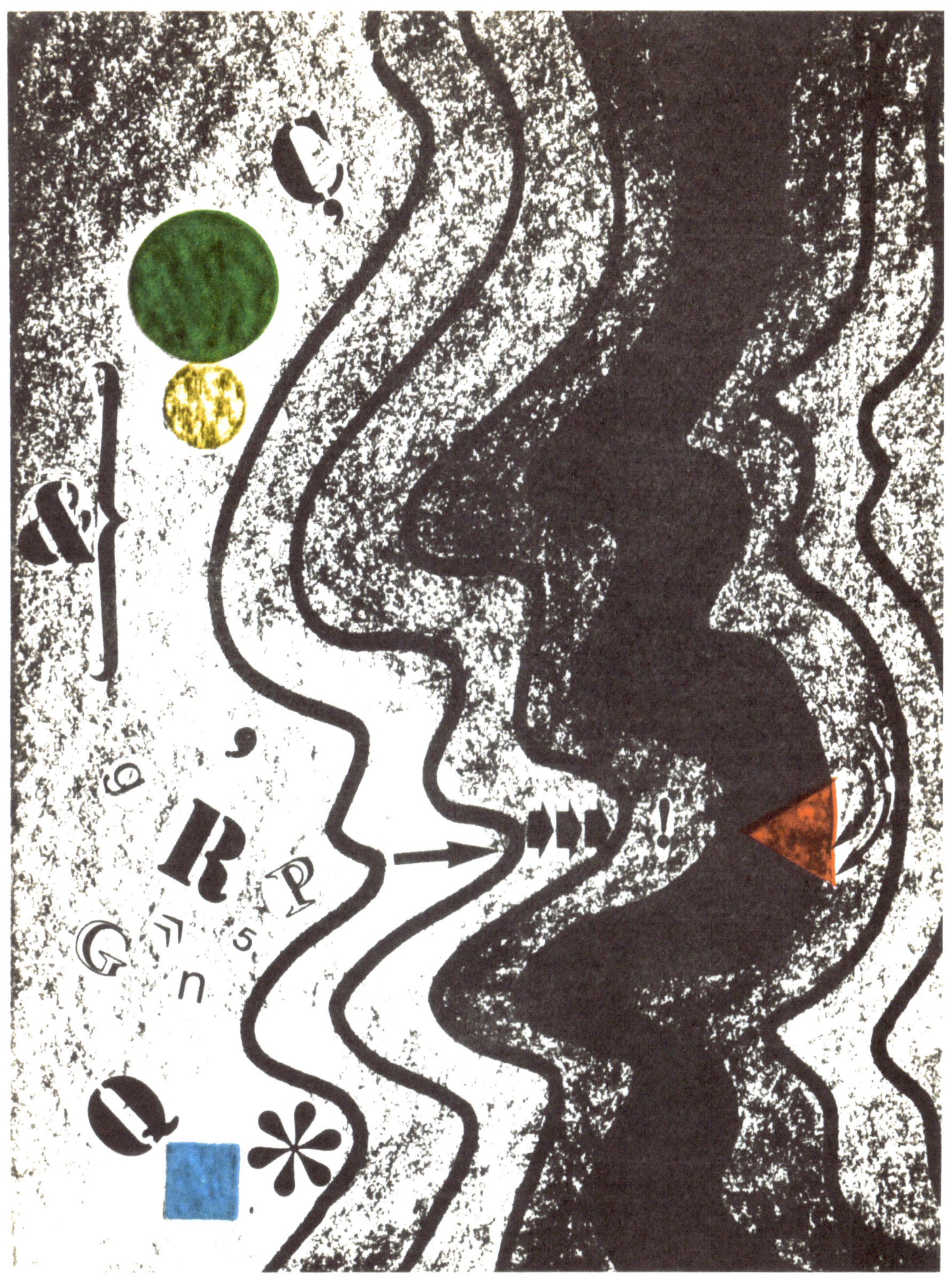

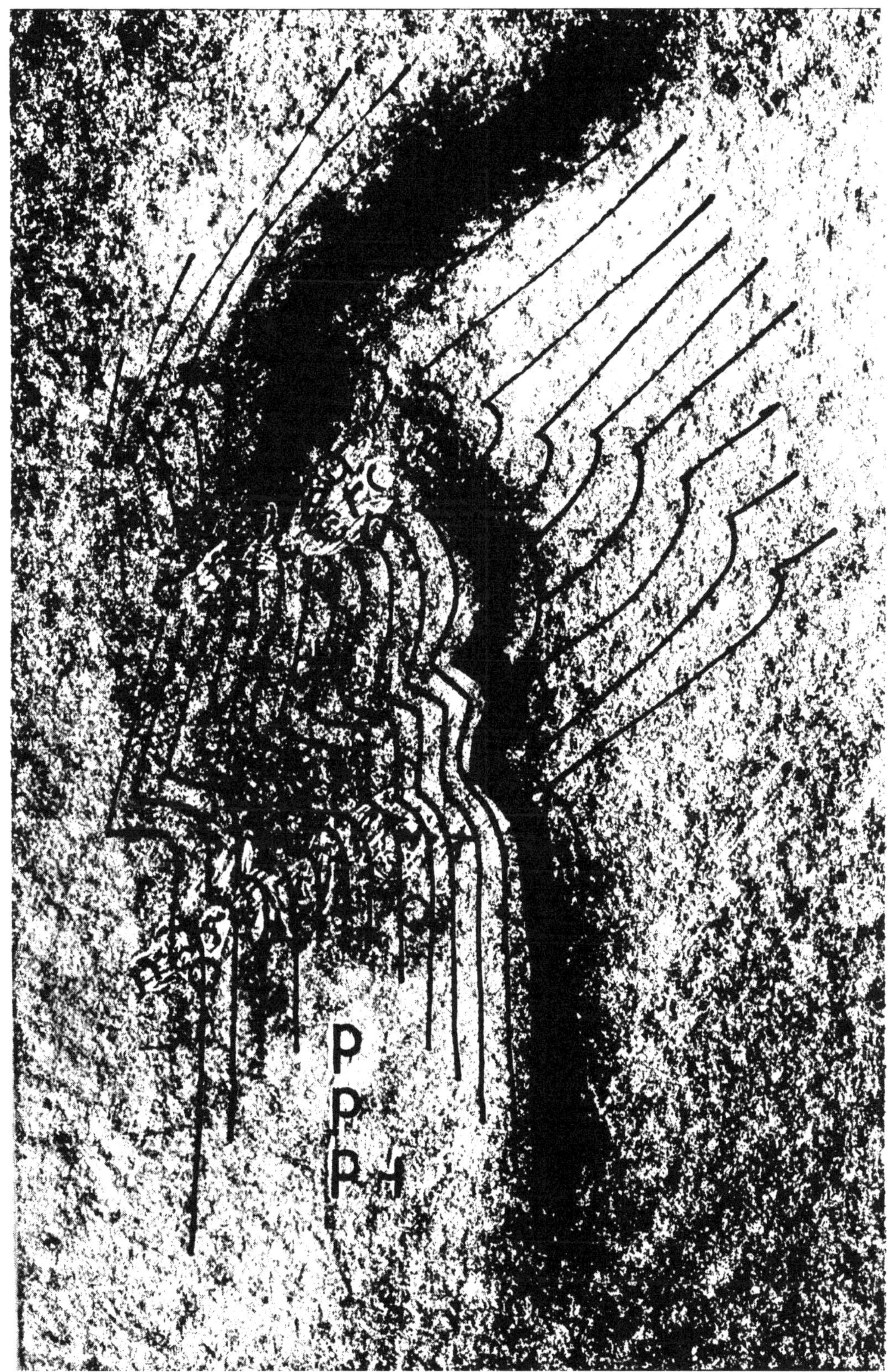

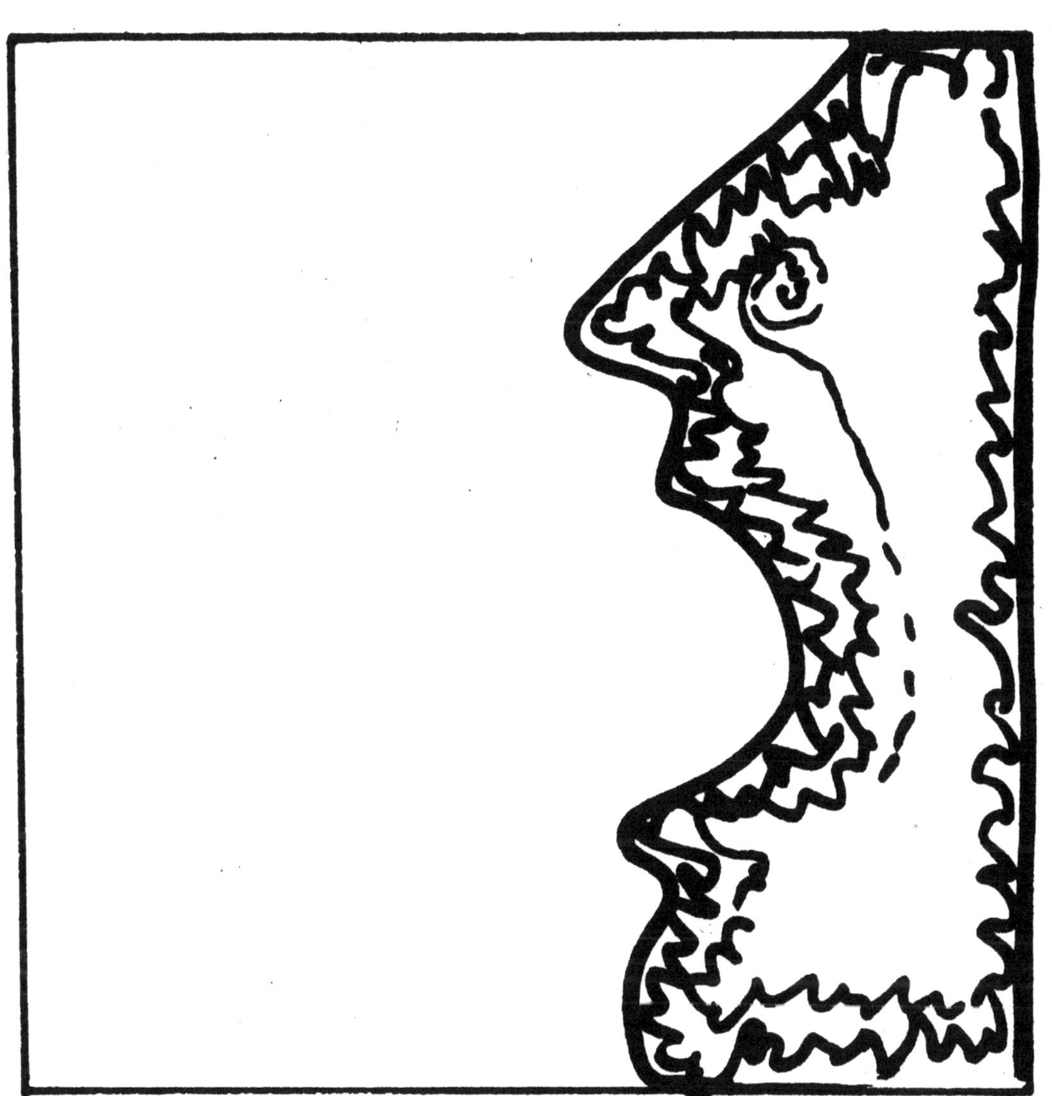

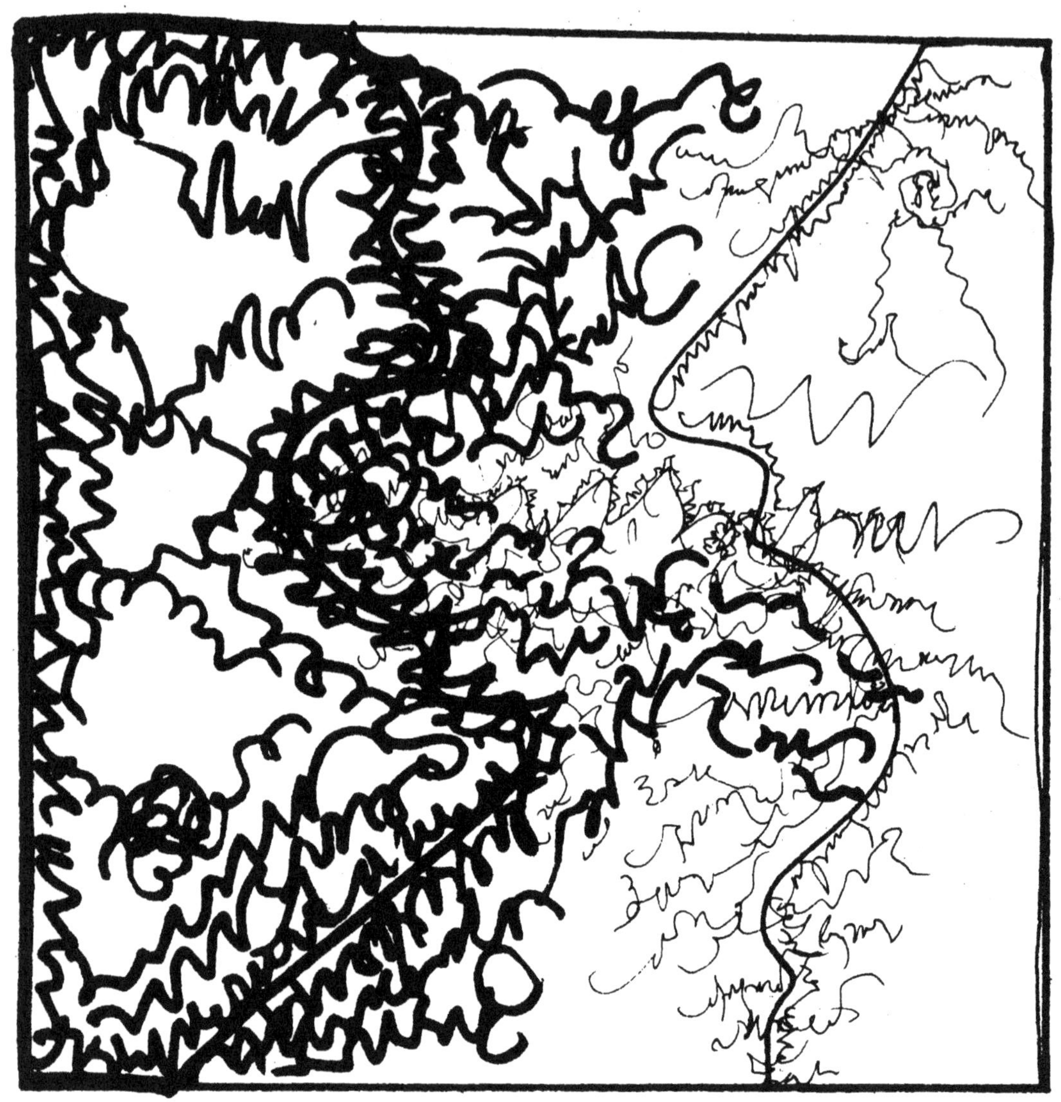

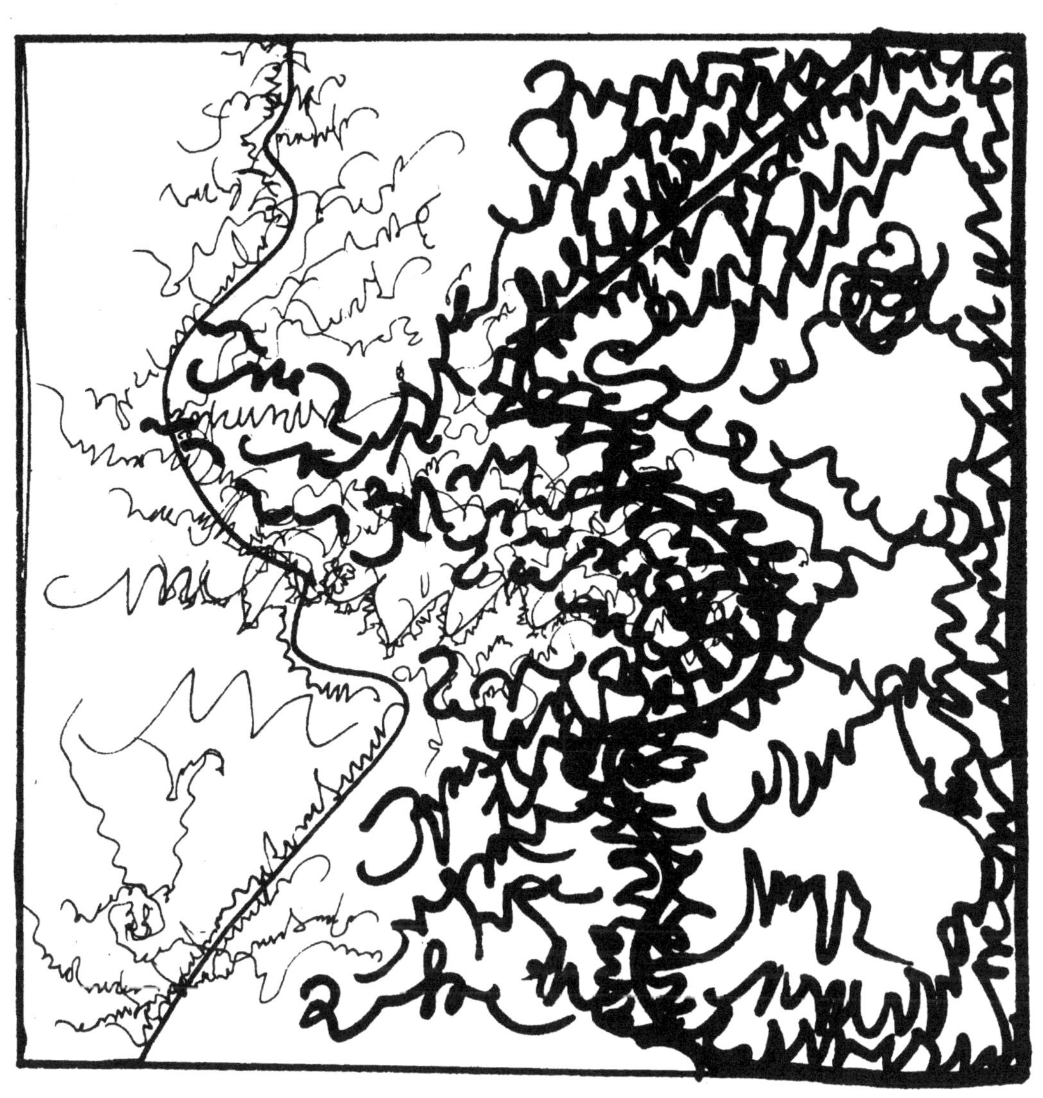

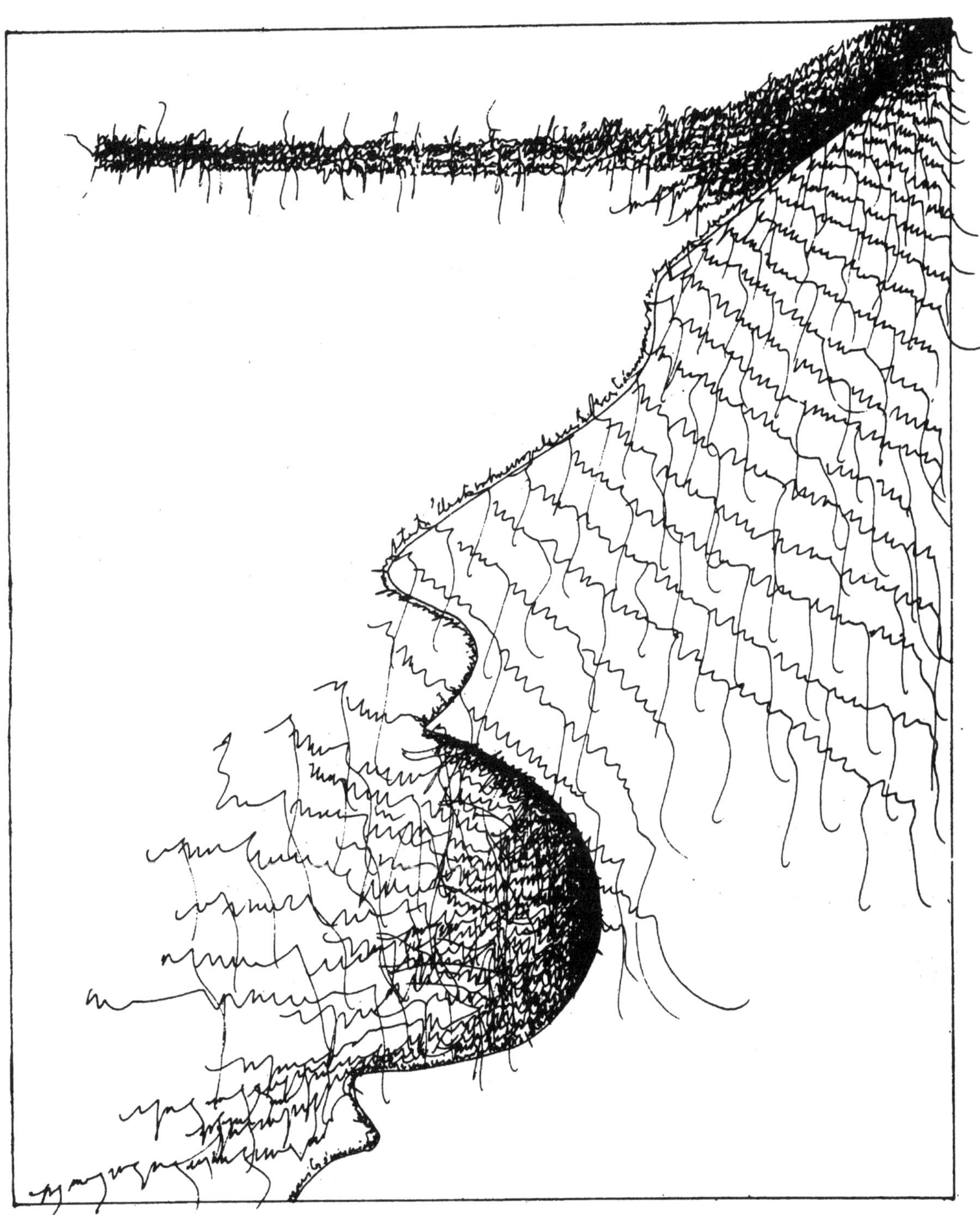

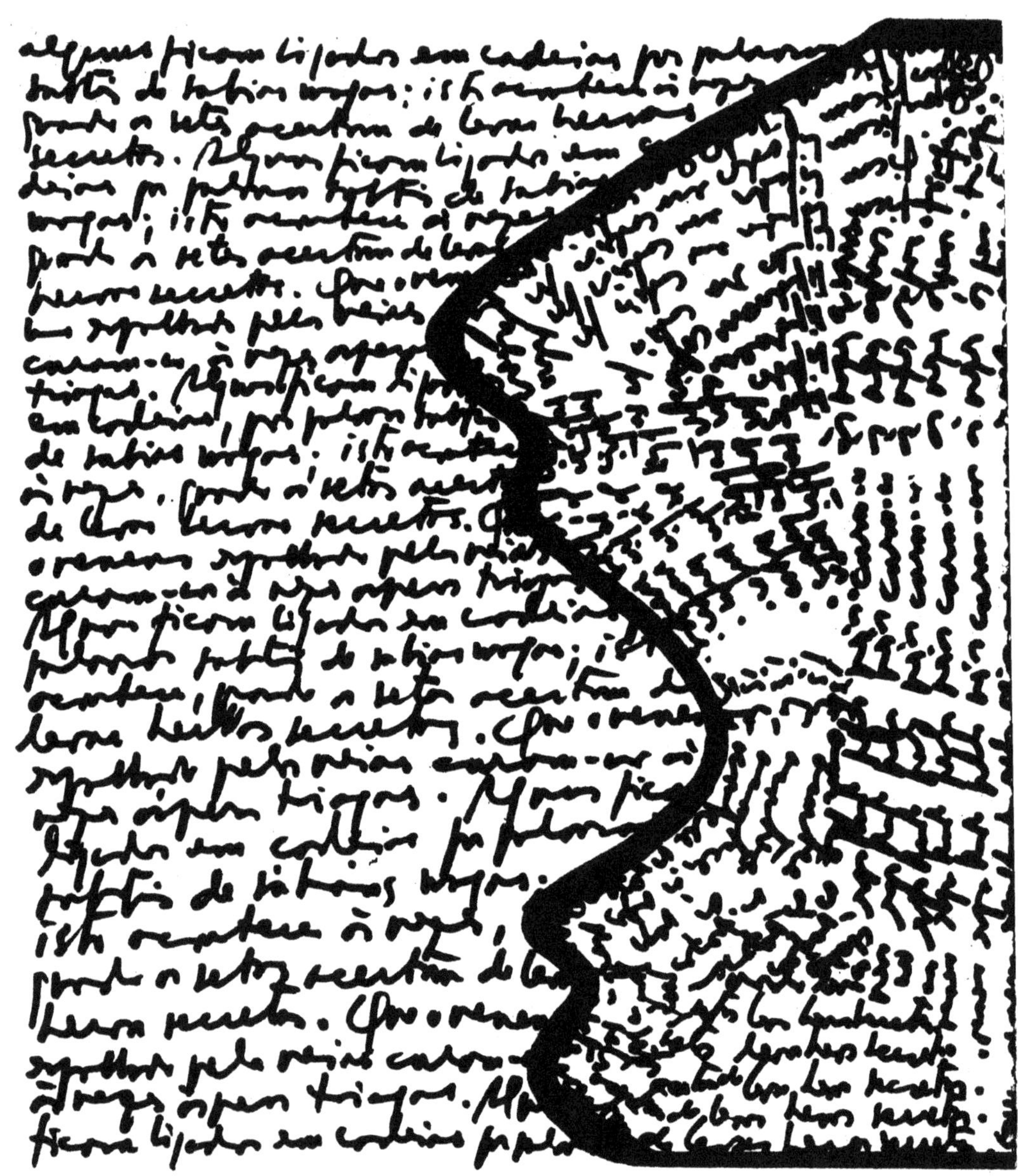

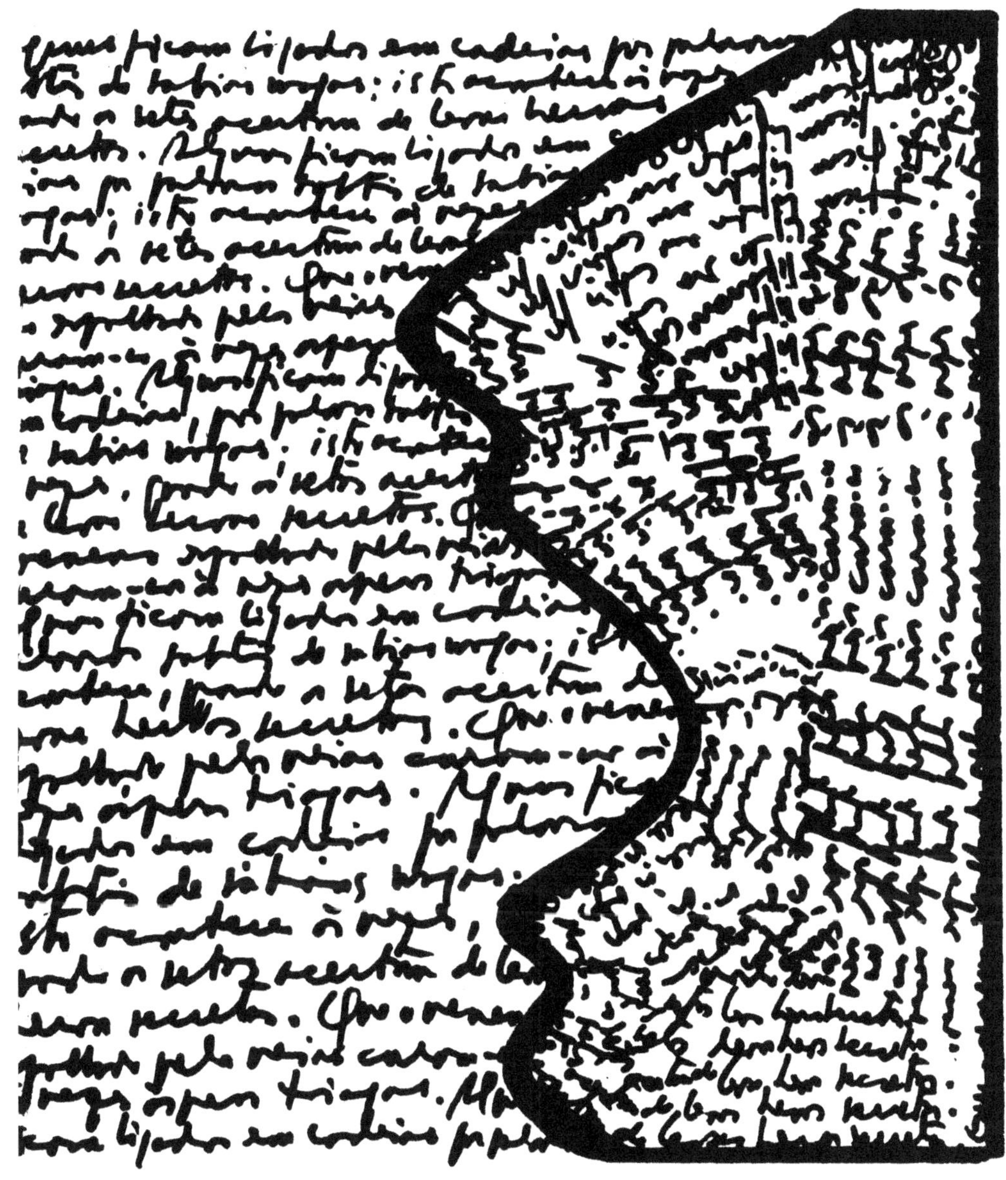

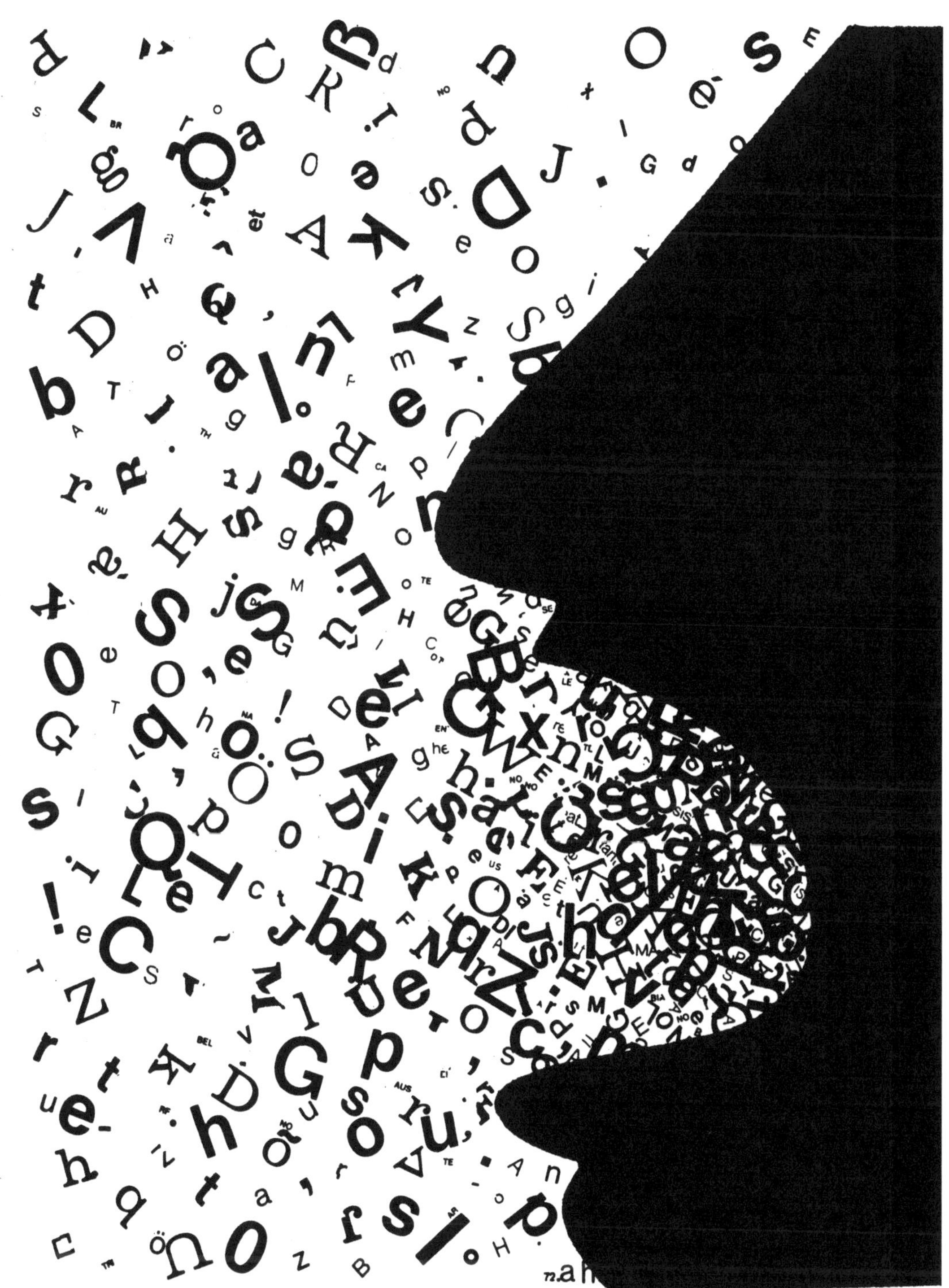

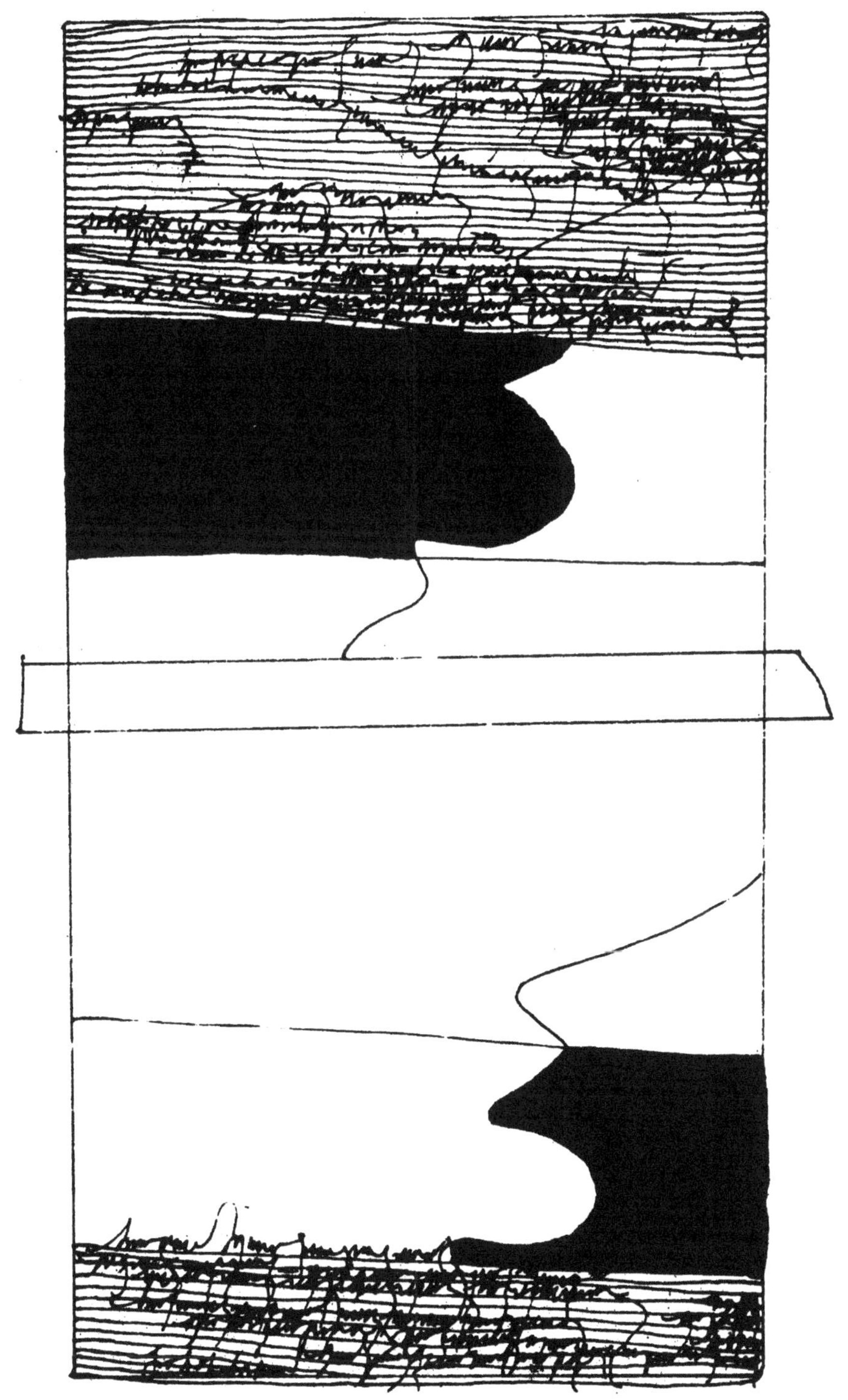

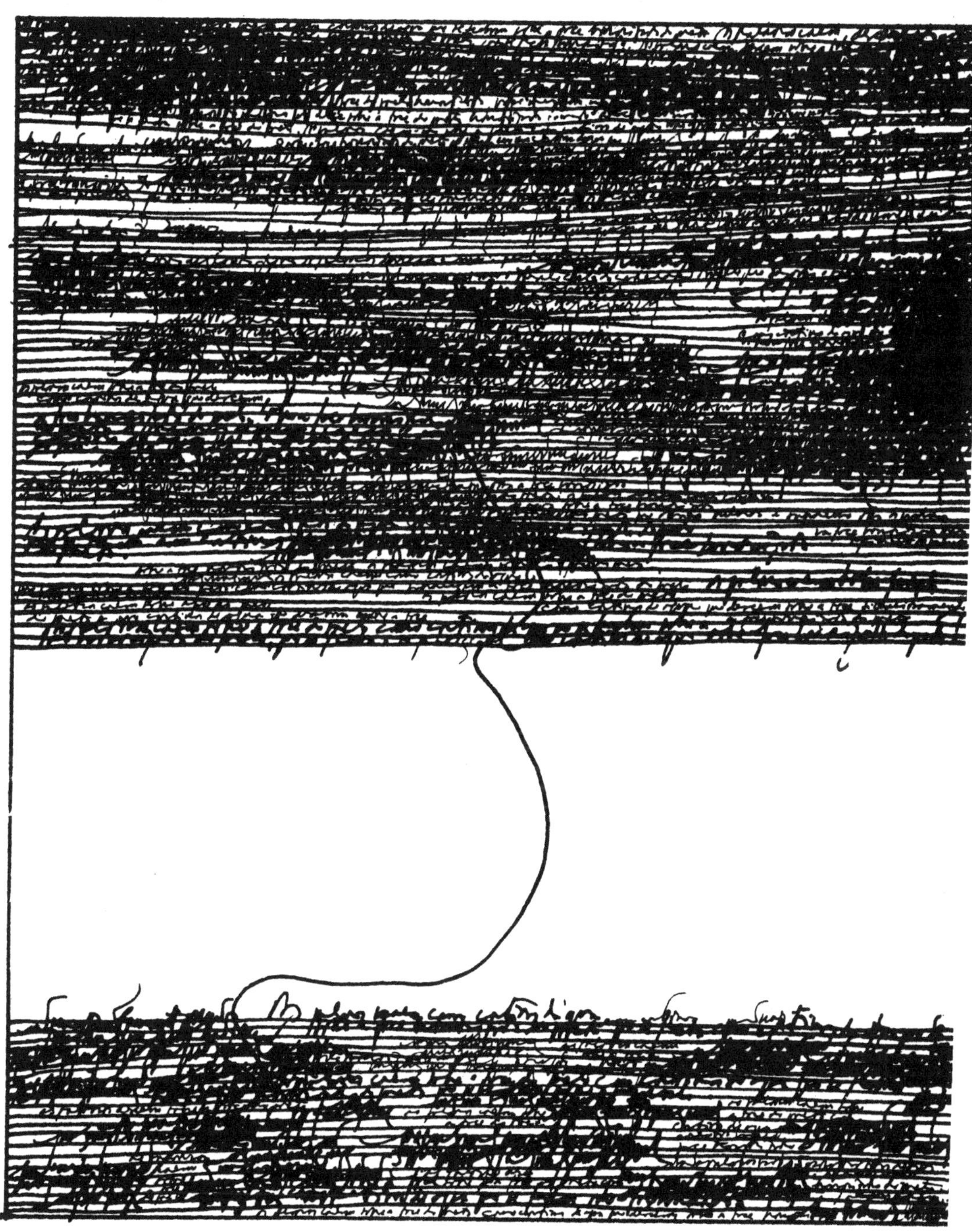

AAAAAAAAA
BBBBCCCCCCC
EEEEEEEEEEE
EFFFFFFFFFF
GGGGGGGG HH
HHHHHHIIIIII
IIIIIIII III   DD;
JJJKKKKKKLLLL
MMMMMMNNN
OOOOOOOOO O
PPPPPPPPPQQQ
RRRRRRRRSSSS
STTTTTTTTTT
UUUUUUUUUUU
UVVVVVVVWW
XXXYYYYYYYZZ
ZZZZ11111222223
4567890&?!ß£$

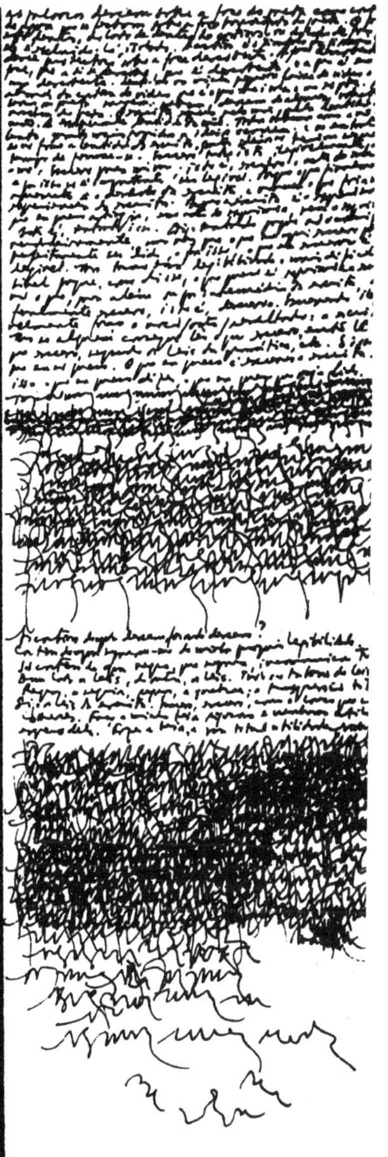

Ana Hatherly was never content to let words remain still. A poet, painter, filmmaker, and one of the leading voices of Portugal's experimental poetry movement, she transformed writing into something far more than a tool for communication. In O Escritur, Hatherly invites us to witness the page as a living surface—where letters drift toward abstraction, where calligraphy becomes dance, where meaning is not fixed but always in motion.

This book belongs to the heart of her lifelong exploration of the boundaries between word and image. From her early poems of the 1950s to her participation in the radical Poesia Experimental movement of the 1960s, and later in her visual art and films, Hatherly pursued one essential question: what else can writing be? O Escritur offers one of her most daring answers.

Here, the familiar order of language dissolves. Instead of sentences, we find gestures. Instead of definitions, we encounter signs that feel both ancient and newly born— at once hieroglyph, notation, and pure invention. Reading becomes a form of looking; meaning arises not through translation, but through rhythm, texture, and presence.

Seen alongside her other major works—such as Anagramático (1970), her explorations of visual poetry, and her later prize-winning O Pavão Negro (2003)—O Escritur is a key to understanding Hatherly's restless creativity. It stands as both book and artwork, part of a larger vision in which writing is liberated from convention and restored to its primal energy.

Ana Hatherly (1929–2015) was born in Porto, Portugal. She earned a degree in Germanic Philology from the University of Lisbon and later completed a PhD in Hispanic Studies at the University of California, Berkeley. Her literary debut came in 1958 with *Um Ritmo Perdido*, and in the 1960s she became a central figure in Portugal's *Poesia Experimental* movement, exploring the intersections of language, image, and abstraction.

From 1971 to 1974 she studied film at the London Film School, returning to Portugal during the "Carnation Revolution". This period marked a turn toward experimental cinema, most notably the short film *Revolução* (1975), which documents Lisbon's post-revolutionary atmosphere. In the following decades, she continued to develop a body of visual and asemic works that expanded the boundaries of writing and calligraphy.

Alongside her artistic career, Hatherly pursued a distinguished academic path. She joined the faculty of Universidade Nova de Lisboa in 1981, where she founded the Institute of Portuguese Studies and became a leading scholar of Baroque literature. She also founded and directed the literary journal *Claro-Escuro* (1988).

Her contributions were widely recognized through exhibitions, retrospectives—such as her 1992 show at the Calouste Gulbenkian Museum—and numerous awards, including international prizes for her 2003 collection *O Pavão Negro*.

Hatherly died in Lisbon on 5 August 2015 at the age of 86, leaving behind an influential body of work spanning poetry, prose, film, and visual art. Her legacy continues to shape contemporary understandings of experimental literature and asemic writing.

Hysterical Books
Asemia Editions

2025

9 780940 821347